SHINING
DARK MA

IAN MEACHEAM

Shining Lights Dark Matters
Copyright ©2018 APS Publications

All rights reserved.
The moral right of the author has been asserted.

No part of this publication may be reproduced, stored in or introduced into a retrieval system, or transmitted, in any form, or by any means (electronic, mechanical, photocopying, recording or otherwise) without the written permission of the publisher except that brief selections may be quoted or copied without permission, provided that full credit is given.

Cover artwork by Alpha Spirit courtesy of Thinkstock

APS Publications,
4 Oakleigh Road,
Stourbridge,
West Midlands,
DY8 2JX

www.andrewsparke.com

I dedicate this book to:

My family and friends

and to the other loving families and friends everywhere who endeavour to keep the memories of those who are no longer with us shining brightly in these dark days.

Contents

Section 1: Poem Poems

First Poem	3
Toilet Poem	4
Fake Poem	5
Abstract Poem No 5	6
Unmadeup Poem No 1	7
Homeless Poem	8
Problem Poem	9
Nameless Poem	10
Advice Poem	12
Fading Poem	13
School Poem	14
Private Poem	15
Flat Pack Poem	16
Recycling Poem	18
Basket Poem	19
Upgrade Poem 1	20
Upgrade Poem 2	21
Ugly Poem	22

Section 2: Proems

Proem	25
Feel Free	26
Long Lost Father	28
Slimming Land	31
Ghost House	35
Man Shopping	40

Man Shopping Again	48
Thrilled by Numbers	49
Muddle Earth	52
Wedding Invitation	54
Christmas Letter #139	60
Job Application	63

Section 3: Sleeping Beauties

Sleeping Beauties	67
To Justine Damond	68
To Victoria Soto	70
To Stephanie Slater	72
To Natalie Ward	74
To Judee Sill	76
To Lidia Dragescu	78
To Christine Keeler	80
To Heather Heyer	82
Last Poem	84

Section 1

Poem Poems

First Poem

I am the first poem
Among equals,
I am the queen of poems
Compared to all of my other subjects.
I have successfully succeeded and over-powered
All other poems that have dared to challenge me.
And now I have been crowned and honoured
With the title
"First."

I am famous and important
Due to my birth right.
I feature in all of the latest publications,
But don't ask me for a quote,
Don't ask me for a pose
As my poetry, as well as my prose
Will cost you in copyright.

So, I will sit here on high,
Looking down at the rest of you
In your lowly positions.
I will sit here on the first page
Smiling and pitying
Your willingness to accept
Your place in the book.
I am the first poem
Among my many subjects.

Toilet Poem

They say there is a poem
In everyone.
Somewhere inside of you.
Well, I have tried and tried,
Strained and strained,
But it just won't come out.

Some people are long winded,
Some have verbal diarrhoea,
But not me,
I sit here and try to pass the rhyme,
But I just can't
Get it down on paper.

Fake Poem

This poem is fake,
I'm afraid I made it up.
I made it up
So that you would read it
And believe that it is real,
A real poem.

But there is no truth here,
My words lie on this page
Tricking you into believing
That this is a real poem
By a real poet
And it is worthy of publication.

I apologise
If this is all fake news to you.

Abstract Poem No 5 – *Ian Meacheam (2018)*

This poem is the fifth in a sequence of nine poems portraying the true value and power of the silence between words. The poet, in a rare interview, explained that "the blank white space **is** the poem as it encapsulates the futility of language. Words, in the end, are meaningless and merely spoil the real message of my poetry."

```
BEDROOMZZ
CLOTHESZZZ
NEWZSHEETSZEMPERORZWINDZDOUBLEZINZPILLOWZSIZEZKINGZSINGLEZ
MODERNZCONZDOMZTALKZSPITZARTZDRINKZPIZZZKINKZFARTYZDRUGSZ
MADEUPMAKEUPUNMADEUNMAKEMADEUPMAKEUPUNMADEUNMAKEMAD
ZZZ                                                                                                          ZZZ
```

Unmadeup Poem No 1 – *Ian Meacheam (2018)*

This piece of poetic art depicts the poet in the first stages of creating a poem. In another rare interview the poet explained that "early in the morning the muse often takes me. I get out of bed quickly and make up poems. This is the first poem in a series of master bed pieces."

Homeless Poem

Please can you spare me some time?
I've been sitting here
On this bleak, blank paper
Waiting for acknowledgement.

Over time
The ink occasionally moved
From one unsafe place
To another.
Never settling, never certain.
No prospects of ending.

I try to shelter in a space
That gives me warmth,
But the drafts keep coming,
And I am left in the cold
At the feet of towering figures.

Over time
The blood freezes the heart.
My health and happiness
No longer part of my vocabulary.
These poor words are consigned
To the cold slabs
Of empty pages.

Problem Poem

I don't have a problem with drinking.
I don't have a problem with drugs.
I don't have a problem with eating.
I don't have a problem with smoking.
I don't have a problem with gambling.
I don't have a problem with dying.
I don't have a problem with lying.
I just have a problem with denying.

Nameless Poem

These words have names.
We hang a name on everything
We give common names to....
Objects, actions, emotions.
Our dictionaries are full of these names.

Words span and spread
Across homelands and beyond borders.
Words may drop in and out of fashion
But our language is shared
Conveying the same meaning and sense,
More or less.

But certain words are left
Unsaid and unnamed,
They are beyond definition,
Beyond belief and description.
These names are left without
Identity and legacy.

These names are people
And they fall by the way side.
Through nameless acts of
Inequality, exploitation, inhumanity.

And some of the rest of us,
Who will remain nameless,
Are left speechless,
Feeling powerless
To name names.

So, we close the book
Or turn a page
And refuse to name the word.

Leaving the world failing us
As all our words fail us
All.

Advice Poem

We point the way
With our wrinkled green fingers,
Sprinkling suggestions
Here and there,
And occasionally the seeds of advice
Sink into the fresh virgin ground.

But the soil dries in time,
The garden groans,
Plants wither to weeds
And return to the land.

My futile autumn world
Looks different
In your fertile green mind.

So, I have stopped planting seeds,
Because I am not you
And you are not me.

But if I were you……

Fading Poem

Many happy birthdays ago
I was bold and bright,
My confident words and thoughts
Jet black and snow white.
I dominated my space and your time.
In the crowd I stood out
Head and shoulders
Above the clouds.
I was sure and certain of myself
Self-assured and growing
Selfish.

Sometime later,
Somewhere, somehow,
My words and thoughts
Lost their certainty and clarity.
They merged and blurred
Into grey ghosts of birthdays past.
I shrank into the crowd
A grim man walking,
As younger types became bold.
And I was left to shed tears from a cloud,
Self-critical and doubting
Self.

School Poem

Mark my words,
This was once
A blank page.

Then my teacher talked to me
And magically it was filled with ideas,
Imagery and beauty.
Mark my words.

And then my teacher marked it.
It was filled with words,
Numbers and grades,
Acronyms, targets
And next steps.

So, I tried to write it again,
But my brain was blank,
As was the page.
Mark my words.

Private Poem

Please, be aware that this poem
Has been privately funded.
Under the contract you have agreed to with the poet
It will cost you extra each time you read the poem.
However, the more you read the poem
The cost will be reduced per reading,
So that in time this poem will appear to be
Exceptional value for money.

Please, also be aware that this poem
Can be upgraded and updated at any time
The poet sees fit.
Consequently, you will have to pay
A service charge,
An annual maintenance fee,
And personal insurance.

At the end of your contract with the poet
You are free to look at other service providers
Who publish this poet's poem.
You can spend many happy hours
Comparing and contrasting
The product with others.
Please, also be aware that this offer
Will not last long,
Nor will this poem.

Flat Pack Poem

Warning!
To assemble this poem
Follow these instructions.
Please check that you are
In a position to read this poem.
You will need to be sitting down comfortably
With the following:

1) A pair of reading glasses
2) A light above your eyes
3) A strong drink.

Before reading the poem
Please also be aware
That you will require
Certain words and figures of speech
In order to construct
This poem.
These include:
Nouns, verbs, adjectives, adverbs,
Similes, metaphors, imagery etc.

Then, check that the text
Is in the right order by scanning the poem
Superficially and quickly.
Once you have done this
You are now ready to read the poem.
For best results, follow these instructions:

1) Read the first line
2) Pause
3) Read the first line again
4) Pause
5) Read the second line
6) Pause
7) Read the second line again
8) Pause
9) Read lines 1 and 2 together
10) Pause
11) Read lines 1 and 2 together again
12) Continue with this process until you reach the end of the poem
13) Pause
14) Read the whole poem again in one go
15) Pause
16) Take a stiff drink
17) Turn off the light
18) Close your eyes for some time
19) Open your eyes
20) Decide which option you would prefer:
    a) Deconstruct the poem
    b) Read another poem
    c) Close the book and donate it to a charity shop

Recycling Poem

When you have read this poem
Feel free to recycle it.

If you think it is rubbish
Just tear it out of this book,
Place it in the correct bin
And it will be taken away.

The recyclers will then
Sort through all of the words
To see if there is anything worth saving.

Maybe, just maybe, there will be a few words
That are worth saying again
In my next rubbish poem.

Basket Poem

Are you sitting comfortably?
Then we can begin.

Search and you'll find,
It's the thrill of your life time.

Please, buy me on line,
It will save you prime time.

Buy me, buy now,
Buy me, buy buy.

It's on its way today,
Now that you've paid.

Please, tell all of your friends,
It's the thrill of your time line.

Are they sitting comfortably?
Then they can begin.

Buy me, buy now,
Buy me, buy buy.

Upgrade Poem 1

Sorry to stop you there,
But before you read this poem
Please shut down this book
And then open it up again.
Our records show that
This poem needs an upgrade.

The poem was working perfectly well
In 2017.
But unfortunately
In 2018
It needs updating.

You may also find that other poems
 In this book
Are not working as efficiently
As they should be.

So, our advice is to upgrade all of the poems
By buying the latest version of this package.
These upgrades are available now.
Working on updates
30% complete
70% complete
100% complete
For now.
Don't turn off your book.

Upgrade Poem 2

We need to remind you that
Your subscription to these poems
Is coming to an end
And you are required to
Upgrade this anthology. **Click here to install.**
We have added some new features
Which we know you will like.
These additions will make reading
These poems faster and easier. **Click here to install.**
You may experience
Some teething problems
Using the updated anthology.
Don't hesitate to contact us
On our 24-hour helpline and
We guarantee to answer you
Within 24 hours. **Click here to install.**
You will, of course, be frustrated
That you have just got used to the last update
And now we are telling you that you must
Change your way of operating,
But give it a year and you will
Have mastered the upgrade. **Click here to install.**

Your annual upgrade is just
One click away. **Cock her$ to **stall,**

Ugly Poem

I know my place,
I am on my own,
Because I am an ugly poem.

All the other poems
Are grouped together.
They are all tightly arranged
Looking for admirers.
And when they are out in public
People will look at them,
People will study them,
People will talk about them.
But not me,
I am an after-thought
Tagged on the end.

Once upon a time
I sat next to a beautiful poem.
Was that because there was
Only two of us?
Or was it to make the other poem
Seem more attractive?

But now,
I am on my own,
I know my place.
I am an ugly poem.

Section 2

Proems

Proem

I write proems.
I'm not a poet,
I don't write prose.
I'm a proet of sorts.
Sometimes
I write words,
Sometimes phrases,
Sometimes sentences,
With my short hands
And sometimes with my long hands.
I pray, one day that
I have something to say,
But my words don't scan or rhyme,
They are never in the right order
And they don't contain a message.
They are too short for prose,
Too long for poems.

So just call me a proet,
Please read my proems.

Feel Free

BE FREE, BE WORRY FREE.
BUY THE NEW PERSONAL SECURITY OFFENSIVE FORCE FIELD.
YOU WILL NEVER HAVE TO WORRY ABOUT ANYONE EVER AGAIN.
NO-ONE WILL BE ABLE TO INVADE YOUR PERSONAL SAFE SPACE.
JUST STRAP IT ON TO YOUR BODY AND CONNECT TO THE WIFI
AND SWITCH ON THE ALARM.
NO MORE UNWANTED HUMAN CONTACT.
THE PSOFF COMES IN THE FOLLOWING POPULAR SIZES – SMALL OR MEDIUM
(No need for the larger sizes - for obvious reasons)

ONLY £499.99!

BUT THAT'S NOT ALL!
BUY THE NEW PSOFF AND GET A SET OF THE LATEST PERSONAL SECURITY EAR DEFENDERS ABSOLUTELY FREE.
STOP ANY VERBAL ABUSE OR HARASSMENT-
NO MORE SEXISM, RACISM, AGEISM, GENDERISM AND MANY, MANY MORE!
JUST ADJUST THE SETTINGS FOR YOUR OWN PREFERENCES

OR GO FOR THE SILENT MODE – FOR ABSOLUTE SECURITY AND SAFETY!
REMEMBER - IT'S YOUR FREE CHOICE TO BE OFFENDED!

BUY THE NEW PSOFF AND GET THE NEW PSED ABSOLUTELY FREE.

FEEL FREE FOLKS!

Long Lost Father

Somewhere between his death and my birth, I lost my father. Not in a busy shopping centre. Not in a mental institution. And not in a game of poker. It was more gradual and insidious than that. But I don't know when the loss started and I don't know how and, most significantly, I have no idea why.

As his son, I wasn't perfect, I never was or am. Not even close. We were not close then and we are certainly not close now. I'm sure all children say that about their parents. It is in our young genes to biologically and psychologically disagree and dislike your parents at times. At some point parents' usefulness wears thin as our independence or perceived independence grows stronger. Peers outweigh parents. Rebellion out trumps conformity. Novelty and difference exceed experience and normality. So, we move slowly across the spectrum from total dependency and love towards a grudging and begrudging obligation of caring, pity and resentment. We convince ourselves whilst on this slow and painful journey that we will perform better as parents. We learn from them by listening and looking at their faults and flaws. And we make judgements, muttering and murmuring to our nearest and dearest of roughly the same age group as to why our parents are not what we wanted or wished for. As if we had a choice. We say to our trusted friends "you can choose your friends but not your family," knowing full well that some of our friends have a "best before date." Our parents, on the other hand, have a life-long warranty.

This special and difficult bond between parent and child is often shared and consequently confused by another parent or other siblings. The long-life mother's milk is diluted by all of these other stakeholders. At birth we latch on to the mother for succour and comfort and try to ignore and dismiss the other distractions with an occasional smile, kiss or hug with other family members. But the one that misses out is the old man.

The new and modern father may fight for equal rights while hunting for and trying to gather in a new role but somehow and somewhere he is left out in the cold. Consequently, the father has to create a new role for himself – a voice of reason, a hand of practical help and a bullet-proof chest. In time the father figures out that his real purpose on this planet, the most precious employment given to Man, is a series of part-time menial jobs – painter, decorator, mechanic, bank teller and taxi driver. He loses himself in amongst his man's work and then slowly in time, the ties that bind, loosen with his own child.

The father loses his grip on his tools and before long the child is lost. The years roll by and his child grows, the father slowly out-lives his use in these roles. Younger, more credible and trusted workers take his place.

This is how it was with my father. He lost his jobs and there was nothing left for him to do. He couldn't build book cases anymore. He couldn't show his feelings anymore – neither good nor bad. No building of bridges - no displays of affection, no words of love. My father was retired off and was left on the side lines, passed his cell by date, out of touch and out of range. He placed himself in solitary confinement without a care in his world. And his world shrunk and revolved around himself and no-one else.

And I look back to find out the moment it changed and I can't see or feel it. But it happened somewhere, somehow. I tried to stop the family cycle almost as soon as my father had taught me how to ride my bike. "I will be different", "I will do a better job", "I will show my feelings towards my child," I cried, freewheeling away. Away from my proud father.

We are now miles apart. Wasn't the agreement that parents love you whatever, no matter what you think of them? Isn't that what unconditional love is supposed to be?

But the inevitable happens. Love turns to hate and then to indifference. And the passion and intensity of a hopeful love story turns into a domestic soap opera of tears and fears before ending in a post-apocalyptic barren wasteland. And the audience leaves the show of our lives feeling sadness, guilt and shame.

My father has lost me, I have lost my father and I have lost myself.

Slimming Land

It is midday.
I have not eaten since 7.38 pm last night.
I am cold.
I am wearing only light trousers and a thin tee-shirt.
My stomach is rumbling.
I am hungry and nervous.
I am about to enter the Land of Slimming.
An over-populated world of fatties.

"Hello all, come on in, form a large queue."
An unfortunate choice of words, I think.

We wait in turn to pay our weekly subscription to be a member of Fat Club.
First rule of Fat Club - don't call it Fat Club.
Some are happy to be here. It is the only time in the week when they can relax and be larger than life in the company of other non-judgementals.

Some would be happy to be here if it wasn't for the pizza and chocolate cake that they had for breakfast this morning.

Some are not happy to be here at all. I am one of this group of fatties who hates the whole experience and right now would prefer to be anywhere else. But I have to come here, I need to be judged and I need the prospect of disappointment, embarrassment and humiliation.

So, I stand in line, shuffling forward towards the judges' desk. My membership card in my sweaty over-weight hand. I attempt to avoid eye contact. I try to look down at the floor only to see my fat stomach and the fat ass of the person in front of me blocking the view.

If I were to look around me I would confirm what I already know. I am the only man in the queue. In any other setting this would be a gift from heaven for some men. But as a bald, old, fat fart I am not turning any heads. The sisterhood of women seems to be intent in giving warmth, comfort and protection to their own sex. They talk and joke, they pass the queueing time by sharing experiences and recipes. I keep my head down feeling left out in the cold. A cold sausage sandwich.

The front of the queue is approaching as we slowly march towards judgement day. In my dream-like trance I can see and hear the march of the elephants, Dumbo-style.

"Hello Ian, have you had a good week?"

I want to say to the judge, jury and executioner that I have had an amazing week, I climbed Everest, swam with dolphins, learnt to ski and broke the world record for the 800 metres. But she was basically just asking how much food I had shovelled down my throat. Not to tempt fate, I reply in a non-incriminating way.

"OK, I think…."

As I delivered this detailed and thoughtful response my mind was rewinding meal times over the last seven days, followed by the times between meals where I also ate and drank too much. If I was counting sins or calories I would have run out of chocolate fingers and toes after the first day since my last weigh-in.

I hand my membership card and money over and move along the line towards the weighing scales. It is at this point that the queue spaces out for the following reasons:

1) Even those people who think they have lost weight start hesitating and slowing down as the scales loom larger.
2) The protocol of the personal humiliation is that, to lessen the embarrassment, the person behind does not get too close to the one being weighed so that they can't hear the creaking of the scales and the groaning and moaning of disappointment.
3) As you arrive at the scales you need a few seconds to shed as many items from your body as you can decently get away with. It feels like airport security as shoes, belts and earrings are abandoned, loose change is jettisoned, unwanted hair is removed and false teeth are placed in the glass beaker provided.

It is my turn next. Unfortunately, I hear the pronouncement given to the lady in front of me.

"You have gained three pounds. Any idea why?"

I then wait for a couple of minutes while the woman tries to justify her gross over-eating habits by firing off a series of excuses that the Slimming Land lady reading the scales has heard so any times before. I hear "surprise birthday party, constipation and lack of salad at the corner shop" feature during her long-winded justification. While she explains away her sinful week she unashamedly struggles to dress herself again – her socks, knickers, bra, leggings and shirt are back on and she promises to do better next week.

She leaves the stage and it is my moment in the spotlight now......

I surrender my Slimming Land Diary to the scales lady. Her job is not just to read the scales but record my weight with pluses and minuses. It is not the most technical job in the world but it must feel like one of the most powerful.

I remove every conceivable piece of carry-on luggage I can before boarding the scales. There is 1.5 seconds worth of silence that feels like an hour and a half before I hear...
"One pound."

I stand there dumbfounded and motionless, not so much awaiting a second opinion but because I need a more detailed explanation.

"Do you mean I have gained a pound or lost a pound?"
"Oh sorry, you have lost a pound, well done Ian."

I smile and remain silently smug. Phew! No need to justify my lazy lifestyle this week, no need to explain away those comfort-eating cream cakes. I got away with it. I am a free man again for a few days. Free from free foods. I can sin again!

I leave Slimming Land behind for another week. But my fat behind will be back next week. Maybe fatter or maybe not...?

Ghost House

"Sorry to disturb you, can I interest you in some of these...."
"Surprise! I guess you weren't expecting us..."
"Is it OK if you sign for this parcel for your neighbour..."
"Trick or...."
"Mr Simms, I am DI Murphy, may I come in?"

"Come in, come in, as you can see
This once beautiful house needs a little TLC,
I know the decor looks tired
But it's only superficial,
Before long you could magically turn
This house back into a home,
It just needs the personal touch
And some colourful imagination
Sprinkled around the rooms......
Shall we start with the kitchen?"

"TLC indeed! How dare he!
We had some great times here, didn't we Edith?"

"We certainly did George.
Our one and only true home.
We brought up our son here.
Watched him grow,
Until we left,
Until he left us."

"Now it's time for another family
To make their memories, Edith."

"If you don't mind me asking
What happened to the previous owners?"

"An elderly gentleman had been living here
For a while after his wife died
And then he passed away last year.
I don't know any more details."

"Yes, he does, doesn't he George?"

"Well, he'll know some of the basic details, Edith,
But I'm not sure he will want to say any more."

"The kitchen does need some money spent on it,
New units, appliances, flooring, lighting,
But it has possibilities, you could even extend…"

"I liked our kitchen just the way it is
It suited us, didn't it George?"

"Yes, it was cosy and simple, Edith.
A bit like us!"

"It smells musty, how long has it been vacant?"

"According to my records about fifteen months
It's been on the market for about six months.
I believe the couple's son
Was thinking of keeping the property,
But then things changed."

"I'm not surprised he didn't want to live here.
Too many bad memories!"

"Now don't go on George,
It's not his fault he can't live here,
We must take some of the blame."

"This is the largest bedroom
I know there is no en-suite
But if you knock down this wall
And bring the services from the bathroom
Then it would be quite possible."

"Why would anyone want another bathroom upstairs?"

"It's all the rage now, you're showing your age George!"

"How old am I anyway, Edith?"

"How would I know George, I stopped counting
When I stopped……"

"I'm sorry Edith, I didn't mean any harm."

"It's too late for an apology now George,
It's been said and done."

"There's a strange atmosphere in this bedroom
It feels colder than the rest of the house.
There's a chill running down my back."

"It may be that the windows need replacing.
I'm sure the son would consider a reduced offer."

"I'm sure he would, don't you Edith,
He just wants to get rid of the house

And all of its memories."

"Can you blame him, George, he needs the money."

"And whose fault is that, Edith?
He made some very bad decisions."

"Well, he's paying the consequences now,
He won't be out for another ten years or so."

"It serves him right, it will drive him mad.
He has always been impatient and head strong."

"That's because he takes after his father, George!"

"That's not fair, Edith!"

"Fair! Fair! You don't know the meaning of the word!
He took your life after he discovered
That you took my life.
Now that's fair!"

"I take your point, the garden is small
 But it is secluded and safe,
Very good for young children."

"Is anyone else interested in the property?"

"Not presently, there have been several viewings
But no-one has put in an offer.
So, what do you think?
Can you see yourself happily living here?
Can I expect you to put in an offer?"

"We'll think about it, thanks, good bye."

"They won't buy our house will they George?"

"No, not in a thousand years, Edith,
Not while we're still around."

Man Shopping

Life is short. Life is shorter by the year. The years move faster and disappear quicker, year by year. So, with this in mind, why do I spend a considerable amount of my life in shops? I know, I know, I can almost hear you say, my ancient pre-historic ancestral great, great, grandfather spent his whole day hunting for meat that ran away from him, or even worse, ran towards him. Once caught and killed, Ug the Hunter would have to bring his catch back to the family cave without the aid of a bag for life, a trolley and the boot of a car. He would sling his quarry over his shoulder and make his long weary way home in his Ug boots. He definitely wouldn't have enough energy or strength to also pick up and carry some asparagus tips and a full-bodied red wine to go with the meal. Mr Ug would arrive home from his shopping expedition to be met by his admiring other half and their adoring children. Mrs Ug would have the fire ready and have the table laid. She would strip the packaging off the meat, namely the hair, fur, bones and horns, before gently cooking their dinner under a low light for approximately 6.5 hours, basting it occasionally with its own blood and guts. While the meal was cooking Mr Ug would put his slippers on and snooze by the fire. His kids would just sit there staring at the fire because television and mobile phones had not been invented yet. Mrs Ug would stir the pot wishing for a set of stainless steel utensils, a cookery book by the Hairy Bikers and a dish washer. And the same would happen each day because Mr and Mrs Ug didn't have a fridge or a freezer.

To be fair, shopping, eating, breeding and sleeping was all Ug did. He didn't have to get up early to go to work. There were no real jobs around then. No difficult and demanding work like acting in a soap opera or playing professional football. Whereas now, we all have to work very long hours in order to afford the food we eat – unless, of course you are a half decent actor, footballer or perhaps a criminal who steals from food banks.

Now it's a different age, a different world. A world of possibilities where binary and non-binary sexes all have the opportunity to work for a living hell. A shameful world of seeming equality where people's shopping lists differ greatly but a world where anyone can be or has to be a hunter gatherer. So, Mr "modern day" Ug could leave the hunting, gathering and working to Mrs "modern day" Ug as she is emancipated and free from the shackles of keeping the cave tidy. Now it is quite acceptable for Ug to keep an eye on the kids while the other eye takes it in turn to sleep.

I am a new modern man. I believe in equality and parity. So, every so often I will volunteer to hunt and gather and let my wife stay at home to look after the kids. I will write a list on a piece of paper, throw some bags in the back of the car and drive the half mile to the nearest supermarket. I wave goodbye to my family knowing that they appreciate my sacrifice and bravery.

I arrive in the car park and have to park half a mile away from the supermarket entrance as I am not disabled or transporting children. I should have brought one of my brood with me and left them in the car right by the front door of the supermarket. I find a space to park almost outside our house and walk to the trolley park. I fumble around for a coin that will free up one of the trolleys. In the end I make a deal with a charity worker who is shaking a tin in the foyer that if I give him a £5 note he will open the tin and give me a £1 coin for a trolley.

I am now safely inside the supermarket and ready to shop.... but where is my list? Blast! I left it on the kitchen table. No problem for this hunter gatherer. My first stop is to the newsagent section where I buy a small notepad and a packet of 5 biros costing £2.48. It's worth it because I can now write a list of shopping that I need. 12 minutes later I have remembered and written down three things off the original list. That'll do, I will improvise as I go down each aisle. I'm pretty good at remembering where everything is. But then it dawns on me that things are not how I remembered them the last time I set foot in here. It should have been obvious as soon as I wheeled my wobbly trolley towards the fruit and vegetable section. There was a massive pyramid of pumpkins announcing that it is half way through October and various celebratory events were fast approaching.... only x days until Halloween, only y days until Bonfire Night and only z days until Christmas!

Yeah, yeah, what do I care, I foolishly think to myself as I sail passed the pumpkins and aim for aisle 2. But something is wrong. Things have changed. Things have been moved. Where are the baked beans and the marrowfat peas? They've gone. They have been replaced by small fancy dress costumes and masks that are supposed to scare adults at their front doors so that they will give the little monsters a handful of sweets. The whole aisle of canned food has been re-furbished and re-decorated in blood red and black outfits for children to wear for a few minutes on the evening of October 31st.

Now, I'm all for children having a good time but not at the expense of my dietary requirements. I try the next aisle. Not a baked bean in sight. An aisle full of pet food. Cat food, dog food, bird food, fish food, squirrel food, snake food, meerkat food. Why can't we just sell food for human beings in this store? Why can't the other members of the animal kingdom have their own supermarkets? A meerkat market, perhaps?

I move on - still without anything in my trolley other than 4 biros that I don't really need or want. At last, after navigating and steering myself and my over-sized trolley around pedestrians who may have all passed their driving tests but seem incapable of walking in a straight line, I find a familiar area in the supermarket. The chilled and frozen aisles of milk, butter, yoghurt, cheese, oven-ready crinkle-cut chips and authentic Italian lasagne. There is so much to choose from and so little time as hyperthermia sets in quickly if you hesitate. I should have brought gloves. I throw in the trolley a tub of a butter/margarine substance that informs me that it may or may not be butter or margarine but that it tastes better than either of these and has half the calories and is amazing for my cholesterol. I'm sure this is quite re-assuring for many shoppers but it was never my intention to eat the whole tub in one go. But now that I know that this yellow plastic box of ready-to-spread substance is good for my health I may put it to the test. I also dump a pack of frozen chips in the trolley which means that I am now up against the clock. I have got to finish the shopping, pay for the shopping, pack the shopping in bags for life, find the car, find the nearest trolley park to the car, find the car again and drive home before the chips defrost. I stand there, frozen, deliberating my predicament. Should I place the bag of chips in the trolley now or go back for them when I have placed everything else in the trolley to save on de-frosting time or should I just buy a bag of potatoes from the vegetable section? Mind you, that would mean winding my way back through the ever-increasing traffic towards the pumpkins at the start of the shop. It could be well into November by the time I get back there. So, I opt for the frozen chips and journey on.

My trolley has now got a few items in it but I am trying to increase my pace so that I do not arrive home with a bag of soggy chipped potatoes. This is hampered by a new breed of shoppers. These are the employees of the supermarket who are steering huge trolleys that you need HGV licences to control. These uniformed drivers are slowly making their ways up each aisle collecting goods and depositing the items in various online shoppers' bags. Ironically these are the same minions that earlier in the day were stacking the shelves and now they are taking the goods away. In this modern day mad world, lazy armchair shoppers are selfishly preventing everyone else hunting and gathering because they have ordered a fleet of pantechnicons to collect their food and drink, and in doing so block every aisle inside the supermarket.

I eventually steer my way through the road blocks in my sensibly-sized trolley and head for the bread aisle. I can almost smell the aroma of the freshly baked bread at the far end of the supermarket. I turn the next corner and get ready to accelerate up the aisle with my trolley. I feel like an F1 driver on the starting grid cheered on each side of the track by packs of all sorts of bagels and unappetising rows of thinly sliced angular loaves in plastic bags – each bag claiming that the contents will last longer, even if it will never taste like bread. But the real hot bread is at the finishing line at the end of the aisle, hand made by people in white overalls and silly white hats. I can almost feel the trophy, warm and comforting to touch. But no, where has it all gone? It has all been moved. Aisles 8 & 9 are no longer the domain of white, brown, granary and multi-seed. The shelves are now stacked with Christmas crap. The God of Shopping decrees – "Don't worry about your daily bread, it is getting dangerously close to December 25th, only about eight weeks away, and you must turn your immediate attention from buying important stuff like food to the latest piece of plastic for a sprog to play with for about 5 minutes before it breaks or a hilarious knitted jumper with Rudolph's nose flashing while the battery lasts." I detour as I despair and follow my nose to the bread which has been demoted to aisles 14 &15. I grab a warm loaf and position it well away from the cold chips. More incentive to get home quickly – the chips need to be revived in the freezer and the bread needs to be sampled while still warm and eased down my throat with a delightful smearing of the healthy yellow substance I have also just picked up. I can't remember what else was on the shopping list at home but I have hunted and gathered more than enough supplies for the family to feast on. We could have beans on toast or chip butties. A feast for any modern family.

I head for the tills. I am not alone. There are queues and decisions to be made. Do I risk the self-service area and going into meltdown and probably smashing the talking screen with my semi-frozen chips as it tells me that there is an "unauthorised object in the bagging area"? Or do I go to one of the tills with a human being sitting at the end of the queue who is poised to talk to you from a script. I have a choice here. My first decision is do I join the "Basket Only" queue. Do I qualify for this? I have only got a few items. Should I find a basket and transfer my goods into the basket and head for that small queue? But I can't find a basket, so I try the next quickest thing, the "10 items or less" queue. But how many items do I have? I count them and then to re-assure myself I count them again. I have dismissed the 4 biros in the pack of 5 as I bought them separately, so I guiltily take them from the trolley and slip them in my pocket. Why do I feel guilty? I have paid for them already and I have the receipt.... Somewhere. Oh God! Where did I put the receipt? Found it, panic over. Anyway, the can of baked beans I am counting as one item, not 57, which it says on the tin. I count and re-count the rest of the trolley and get to 12 items each time. What do I do now? I know, I'll get rid of two items. How about the two bars of chocolate I bought as a reward for myself for volunteering to do the shopping? No-one was going to know that I had eaten the chocolate because it would have conveniently disappeared before I got home along with the receipt for the shopping. But I need the chocolate and the rest of the stuff is for our meal tonight. So, I have to go to one of the longest queues. Which one do I choose? There are complicated decisions still to be made here. To get home as quickly as possible, do I go for the quantity of stuff on the conveyor belt at each till or do I go by the quality of the people? By quality I really mean one of the following:

1) Who is the most lonely-looking shopper in front of you as this will inevitably involve a lengthy conversation with the till operator?
2) Which operator looks bored and wants a chat with the customer about each item they have bought?
3) Which shopper looks as if s/he has picked up an item without a price or barcode on the product?
4) Which operator is new and doesn't know what s/he is doing?
5) Which shopper wants to use every possible voucher and loyalty card in order to save 7 pence from the bill?
6) Which operator needs to change the till roll and the ink cartridge as the receipts are not at Fleet Street quality?
7) Which shopper has forgotten to buy something and the queue has to all wait while they go and collect a pumpkin?

I weigh up my choices and decide on a queue and I wait. The queue gets shorter, as does my life. I eventually place my 12 items on the conveyor belt and the goods that I have fought bravely for are moving slowly towards a chap on scanning duty. Surely, we won't have to talk to each other? Please just let me pay and put my shopping in my bag. As the shopper before me in the queue wheels away while saying her goodbyes, I check that I am prepared. I have my wallet and a bag. I am at the till. Each product scans beautifully, no problems. Check Point Charlie does not speak to me other than asking me if have a loyalty card, any vouchers that may still be valid or if I need help with putting my 12 items of shopping into a bag. I stop myself from making a sarcastic remark or any remark as I don't want to engage him in a conversation. I grunt at him and manage to pay him without the need for any assistance. I have hunted and gathered! I speed towards the exit sign. I park my trolley, sling my bag over my shoulder and trudge back to the car, victorious in defeating the supermarket. And I drive home after quickly consuming the two bars of chocolate.

"Wilma, I'm home," I say triumphantly.

"Well done Fred," she replies sarcastically. "Did you manage to get the asparagus tips for the meal I'm cooking tonight for our guests?"

I drop the shopping bag on the kitchen floor, pick up the shopping list off the table and head back out of the door.

Man Shopping Again

She swipes,
A man appears,
A man appears to be
A friend, a mate, a partner.
The man appears to be perfect
The right size, colour, fit.

But she swipes,
And the man disappears,
And a new man appears
To be better than perfect.
Or is he?
Is he better than the last one?
But she's swiped the slate clean
So, she swipes again
And again.

Thrilled by Numbers

Chapter 1
A mysterious first line that makes you want to............................
Read on to the next line.
It won't make sense, but, you will keep reading............................
By the end of the first chapter you may well begin to understand
Who is who and what is what and then, the chapter........stops....

Chapter 2
A different set of characters, a different time and/or a different place......... an unrelated story? This chapter won't make much sense either and then...

Chapter 3
Back to the same scene as Chapter 1. Add more details. Develop the main characters, some appear to be good and some bad.

Chapter 4
Back to the same scene as Chapter 2. Add more details etc.

Chapter 5
By now in the first four chapters there has usually been a murder, disappearance or strange event to whet your appetite and the appetite of a fairly high-ranking police detective with his or her own personal issues and also a subordinate with her or his own separate personal issues. They often share inter-personal issues with each other such as not trusting your colleague or feeling professional jealousy towards your work partner. Both of these police officers also have a pathological inability to believe a single word spoken by truthful, sincere characters in the story. They will bark up many wrong trees before the end of the story.

Chapters 6 – 17
The next few chapters keep skipping between the two narratives, which very slowly start to mesh together in a rather implausible way. It appears that there are connections between

characters in the odd chapters and the even chapters. These characters often share a dark past. Usually, by this stage in the novel, another character is murdered or dies tragically. S/he is often a good, well-meaning person and the readers will often be surprised and want to read more to find out what is going on. Other readers, however, may choose to read a more straightforward plot in a different book.

Chapters 18 - 24
In this section of the story it is necessary for the police investigators to passionately and obsessively suspect the wrong person for the crime. They will doggedly find every piece of evidence that is possible in order to put the spotlight on an innocent person that was in the wrong place at the wrong time.

Chapter 25 - 32
Odd and even chapters are now completely merged into the present day. The chapters are usually quite short now to add tension and they flip between 1) the good main character who is trying to prove his/her innocence, 2) the murderer who is about to commit another evil deed and 3) the police who are just realising that they have to be nice to each other and work together to solve the crime(s) by the end of the story.

Chapter 33 – 44
By now there is a lot less mundane dialogue and a great deal more action. There is still time for a twist that no-one saw coming. This is followed by confusion by the police and all of the characters in the book. The only people not confused are the author of the novel and the real baddy in the story, who are feeling very smug.

Chapter 45
The police find the missing piece in the jigsaw and have to race against time to catch the villain before the pages of the book run out and into the Acknowledgements section.

Chapter 46
The baddy is caught and arrested or killed by the police or dies accidentally but horribly. The goody, who was being threatened by the baddy, is saved and everyone feels relieved.

Chapter 47
There is just enough time for the police to explain the baddy's motives to the characters who are still alive and care. The police officers are now best friends and make it clear that they would like to work together in the sequel.

Chapter 48
This chapter is set twelve months later when the main good character has recovered from his/her ordeal and is now romantically involved with another nice character from the book. The story finishes with a suggestive sentence or two that point to sex or humour or hope for the future.

Chapter 1
Occasionally, if the author and the publishers are confident about the sales of this book, they might decide to print the first chapter of the next book in the series for you to read. And just as you are enjoying this new story, which is very similar to the one you have just read, it stops.

Muddle Earth

Once upon a mini-series
In a plot of land far, far away,
There lived far too many characters
With very long nonsensical names.
They occupied different areas of a fictional map
At the front of a very big thick book.
Each of these characters was kind, cruel or weird
And as their stories unfolded and interlinked
It became impossible to remember and decipher
Who was who and where you were in the story.
It inevitably meant journeying back in time
To a previous chapter,
Or to the beginning of the book,
Or to the glossary of names.

In this world of mainly dirty, down-trodden peasants
There was always a rich ruler of each territory,
Who wanted to invade other lands.
The rulers would treat the little people badly
To prove how big they were,
But even so the peasants adored and followed their leaders.
These rulers would start arguments and conflicts
By cursing their neighbours with unfathomable prose,
They would stab their enemies in the back or front
Or use random selective magic or unexplained super powers.

Meanwhile, in one or more of the two or three sub-plots
There would be love, violence, sex, dragons and short people,
But not necessarily all at the same time or on the same page.

Also, there would be a poor good-looking goody who was destined to be a monarch
And a cruel powerful baddy who was destined to be dead
By the end of the last chapter.

There were also lots and lots and lots of extras,
Some of these characters would die horrible deaths during the story
Often, just after you had learnt how to pronounce their daft names
And worked out which family they belonged to.

And all of the characters and plots
Would try their best to create mayhem and confusion
Throughout the book until it ran out of ideas.
And just as the goodies and baddies that were still alive
Could see the end in sight,
They had to fight to survive the author's axe
And cling on to the cliff edge of reviews and ratings,
Waiting for a reprieve and a sequel.

The End? To Be Continued?
Perhaps...

Wedding Invitation

Dear Sponsors,
_____ and _____ would love to celebrate their wedding day with you.
The ceremony will be at _____ on _____.

This gives you plenty of time to save up for a new dress, suit, shoes and accessories as we expect you to be well dressed but not as well dressed as us.

As we have everything we need in the house we have been living in for six years, we would ask that instead of buying us tasteless expensive presents that you contribute substantially to our honeymoon in Australia and a deposit for a new house. Our bank details are at the bottom of the invitation.

If you have any dietary requests for the day please fill in the section on the reply slip and we will endeavour to pass these on to the hotel's chef so that he can ignore them.

If you have a favourite piece of music that is of sentimental value please also write down the name of the song and the artist on the reply slip. The fascist DJ that we have booked for the evening disco will only be too pleased to tell you that the song is not on his playlist and that he will only play the songs he likes or wants to play in-between his incomprehensible remarks that only he thinks are funny.

You will, of course, feel obligated to attend either a series of hen or stag events before the wedding in which you may have to lose a day or two's pay in order to spend ridiculous amounts of money on doing ridiculous things in ridiculous places.

On the day of our marriage, do expect to be hanging around and ignored for long periods as you are clearly not very important and will be attending the ceremony to make up numbers or because pressure has been put on us to invite you.

At the service, which we have choreographed and rehearsed several times, we will expect your full attention as we have self-indulgently written our own excruciatingly sickening and over-sentimental vows. We have also chosen our favourite music for you to listen to at various points in the service and religious readings by selected people who will nervously deliver the lines in an undecipherable way.

Please remember, this is our day, we are the only people that everyone is interested in, so do come prepared to introduce yourselves and talk aimlessly with other guests who also feel like spare parts. It is, of course, statutory to compliment the bride and groom on their appearances (particularly the bride) after the service and at every opportunity for the rest of the day. Do take endless photographs of us – there is no charge for this. Feel free to also take photographs of the bridesmaids, the best man, the ushers and our parents and grandparents but please be careful to make sure that we feature in almost all of the photographs and that the rest of the family members and close friends do not dominate the photographs. Do use your discretion when it comes to including ugly people in the pictures as we don't want anything to spoil our special day. The official photographer and video recorder will have a list of people that we would prefer not to feature in any photographs, so please have a word with either of these people if you are unsure. Apologies, in advance, if your name is on the list.

Please be prepared to wait around for all of the photographs to be taken. I'm afraid some of you will be expected to stand behind the photographer getting cold and bored hoping that you may be summoned to be in a group shot at the end of the session.

After this you will be ushered into the banqueting room where you will discover that you will be sitting on a table with total strangers. At the table we ask you to introduce yourself and explain the tenuous link you have with one or both of us. It is probably at this point when you will realise that you may well have been on the reserve list and other guests were not able to attend. It is also at this point that you will realise that you are starving as you haven't eaten anything since breakfast. Please don't worry as the food will soon be served - after the speeches.

The various speeches have been scheduled to last for about an hour and a half. It is expected that you will again listen attentively to all of the amusing anecdotes and stories and laugh and applaud in all of the right places. The wedding planner, standing to the left-hand side of the top table, will prompt you to laugh or clap if you are unsure what the correct response should be. Be prepared for some of the speakers to be over-emotional or drunk as they deliver their lines. This, unfortunately, is out of our control but we will try our best to make sure that the two of us will not be too drunk until the disco afterwards.

After the speeches, the food will be served by young waitresses who will have no interest in catering for your every need, only the cash in hand at the end of the night. It will be pot luck if the steak on your plate is rare, medium or well done despite ordering the vegetarian option. We expect you to eat everything on your plate regardless, as this is costing us £67.00 a head, and not complain about the food or the service as this will spoil our big day. After the inedible cheesecake, cold coffee and cheap champagne for all but the top table, we will expect you to leave the room so that the staff can clear the tables and transform the room into a night club. This will take a couple of hours and while we relax in our hotel room upstairs and change into something more comfortable for the evening, you will be expected to sit in the crowded bar making small talk with other "C" list guests who were also not offered a room in the hotel.

At this point we will enter the room again, to the sound of applause, in our fancy night club clothes, still looking better and more refreshed than everyone else. Obligatory compliments will be paid as we make our way into the centre of the dance floor where everyone can take more photos of our first dance as husband and wife. Then you are free to order drinks at the bar at extortionate prices before sitting down at a table to people watch. There will not be any need to talk to anyone for the rest of the evening as the DJ's music will be so loud that you will not be able to hear yourself think or sleep.

Throughout the evening you will be able to admire the cross section of humanity that has been invited to the wedding. There will be a distant uncle who becomes more and more tired and emotional as the evening drags on. He will become offensive and suggestive to both sexes and all ages. There will be several overweight middle-aged women who think they look good in short dresses with plunging neck lines dancing to some hits from their youth. They will perform on the dance floor on their own or in small groups, believing that they are the centre of everyone else's attention. There will be moments, of course, when the DJ misreads his audience and manages to clear the dance floor with one badly chosen song. This is when the young children will occupy the floor and run around and slide along the slippery dance floor in their best clothes while parents implore them to behave themselves or else.

You will notice that half way through the evening more and more people will start looking at their watches and this will be the cue for excuses to be given as to why they have to leave early. Some suggestions you might use are as follows:

- We have an early start in the morning.
- The motorways are bad at this time of night.
- The dog/cat needs feeding.
- I can feel a migraine coming on.

Please decide before launching your exit plan how many people you will need to inform that you have to go and thank them for a wonderful day. We would expect you to shout goodbye above the music to …. us, our parents and other close family members plus the other people that you have sat with during the day as they have become like dear friends over the last half a day, even if you never see them again.

We do hope that you will join us for the day and accept our kind invitation.

PS – there will be a "Canapes and Cakes" event held at a parents' house after we return from honeymoon where we can spend the afternoon and evening re-living the afternoon and evening of the wedding, as well as the honeymoon, with the aid of endless photographs and more tedious anecdotes.

We do hope that you will join us for this exciting event also.

RSVP

Christmas Letter #139

Dear *xxxxxx* and *xxxxxxx*

Ian is writing this seasonal letter to let you know that it has been another amazing year for the Meacheam family. This printed letter is written mainly in the third person to make us seem more important than you and to save on having to personalise any sentiment inside a Christmas card.

Wow, what a year the Meacheams have had compared to your miserable and dull lives! You may already be aware of some of the highlights of the Meacheam year from social media and the newspapers but if you have missed out on some of our exciting times there follows a summary of our year for you to enjoy and envy.

Where to start? At the beginning of January Ian and Ann moved into our new 12 bedroomed, 6 bathroomed house in 16 acres of land. The Meacheams spent many a happy hour instructing interior designers, painters and decorators on how we wanted them to make the new house into a home.

Ian really enjoys the swimming pool and the study which includes its own kitchen, bathroom and pool table. Ann really likes the cinema and the conservatory with its own hot tub. She spent a good deal of time in her swim wear looking out from the air-conditioned conservatory on the extensive gardens, particularly during the summer season when our young gardener was hard at work. Ian does think that the Meacheams will eventually outgrow this house in the future, particularly when the multi-million-pound contract for the film rights to his first novel is finalised. However, the present house will do for now and is already a step higher on our property ladder.

In February the Meacheams decided to take a break from the house work and jetted off to Switzerland for a fortnight's skiing before flying on to Hong Kong for a shopping trip for a week and then catching some sun in our beach house in California for a month. As I'm sure you can relate, the Meacheams felt like they needed a holiday when they got back to Knightsbridge in May but they wanted to oversee some alterations that needed to be made to the house.

In June Ian and Ann were invited by the Queen for afternoon tea at Buckingham Palace. The Meacheams had a glorious day spending time with the likes of Pippa, Camilla and Elton. Unfortunately for you, we were advised not to make any photographs from the event public. So please take the Meacheam word for it that everyone there enjoyed Ian and Ann's company.

In July the Meacheams took the opportunity to see first-hand how their generous charitable contributions have been having amazing effects in the poorest parts of Africa. It was most gratifying to see and hear how humble and grateful the villagers were. It was an emotional experience that took the Meacheams some time to recover from. So, at the end of the African experience Ian and Ann took a few days out to go on safari. Ian was thrilled to bag both a lion and elephant. The lion's skin is now lying proudly across the living room floor in front of the fireplace and the elephant's tusks have been made into rather nice napkin rings.

On September 1st Ian and Ann bought their latest Audi. The Meacheams do like their fast sports cars and naturally the registration plate followed on in our series – "I AM 36"

In November the Meacheams had a bit of a health scare when one of their horses had a stiff fetlock and couldn't compete at Kempton Park in the scheduled race. You'll all be relieved to know that Major Majesty is making a full recovery and one of our other horses, Lady Luck, won at Newmarket the following week.

The Meacheam children are doing very well at boarding school. We get regular updates on their progress and well-being from the principal of the school. Ian and Ann are very proud of them and a Meacheam get-together is being planned for some time next year.

Talking of next year, the Meacheams are looking forward to Christmas and the New Year and the endless parties they will be invited to. The Meacheams naturally trust that you all will try to make the best of the festive season and beyond.

We must endeavour to catch up in the New Year by some means or another.

Ian & Ann Meacheam

Job Application USA - CV and Letter

PERSONAL DETAILS

NAME	*Johnny Doe Jr*
ADDRESS	*XXXXXXXX, USA*
TELEPHONE	*Burner*
DATE OF BIRTH	*??/??/????*
MARITAL STATUS	*XXX*

EDUCATION
High School – Present Day   *University of Life*

QUALIFICATIONS
'High School – Present Day   *Running and Shooting*

PERSONAL SKILLS
Cleaning guns

VOLUNTARY WORK EXPERIENCE AT SCHOOL
Working in a local gun shop for two weeks

PERSONAL INTERESTS
Hunting and Hurting

REFEREES
1. *Charlton Heston*   2. *Donald Trump*
   National Rifle Association   *President of America*

Explain, in no more than 5000 words, why you wish to join the law enforcement agency.

I have always been very interested in the law. At the end of High school, I was voted "the student most likely to be involved with the law in the future."

I have always been fascinated by guns. As a boy, my father took me hunting every weekend, when he was out of prison.

I believe I have the right qualities to carry a gun. I look tough and react without thinking.

It is my constitutional right to apply for this job.
God Bless America.

Section 3

Sleeping Beauties

Sleeping Beauties

Let sleeping beauties lie
In made up silent stories from once upon a time,
Because now we have to wake up
And give consent to our future loves.
Prince may be charming and would die for you
But it's the sign of the times
That his kiss may miss Cupid's target,
And so the greatest romance never told
May tomorrow be
The finest and fairest fiction or news ever sold.

To Justine Damond (1977-2017)

Justine, after hearing a woman crying out for help late at night, reported the incident to the Minneapolis police force. As she approached the first squad car to arrive at the scene, she was shot and killed by a police officer in the car.

Shots fired.
One down.
In the dark
Justine did her duty as a US citizen.
Dressed for a peaceful night's sleep
She came to the rescue
Of an unknown, unnamed neighbour,
Reporting a potential crime to the police
Armed only with a mobile phone.

In the dark
Justine did her duty as a US citizen.
She addressed the police
Who came to the rescue
Of an unknown, unnamed neighbour,
And was shot and silenced
By her protectors and by the law.

In the dark
Justice was not done.
Law enforcement closed ranks,
Body armour primed,
Body cameras turned off,
As the shots rang out
And into the plain clothes of Justine.

In the dark
The clear glass of truth, liberty and justice
Was shattered once again,
By the people entrusted
To protect with courage
And serve with compassion.

In the dark
A bright light shines in the alley
Outside Justine's Minneapolis home.

But the rest of us are left
In the dark.
Recoiling from the senseless gunshots,
All we hear is the automatic volley
"This shouldn't have happened."
"It won't happen again."
In our dreams.

Sleep in peace
In the dark, Justine.
Shots fired.
Many down.

To Victoria Soto (1985-2012)

Victoria, a teacher of young children at Sandy Hook Elementary School in Connecticut, died protecting her class from a gunman who started shooting students and staff.

Victoria was queen
To her small subjects.
She loved and cared
For each and every one.
She lived in and for
Sandy Hook.
A place of fairy tales
Of magic and laughter
And once upon times.
Victoria loved her life,
She loved children and books,
Their happy endings.
She loved them more than life.

So, one day,
When the lone bad wolf
Came to town,
She stood up and in front
Of her little angels.
In an instance
She was immortalised
By her bravery and love,
Shielding her worshippers
From evil,
Without thought or question,
Her instinct was to protect and serve.
Her life's dream ended.

No happy ending.
Just the sound of silence.

Days passed,
Other stories were written
By the truthers and the liars,
By the theorists and deniers.
The conspiracy was spun,
The good was undone.
It became a tale
Of defeating evil with evil,
Gun with gun.

And Vicky's memory was lost
Along with her colleagues
And their children.
And the war of truth and words
No longer centred on casualties
But on the right to bear arms.

The queen was dead,
The queen is still dead,
And our good and true memories
Fade and fail us.
Shame on us all.

To Stephanie Slater (1967-2017)

Stephanie, an estate agent, was kidnapped at the age of 25 and held in a cramped wooden box for eight days. She died at the age of 50 after a short battle with cancer.

She sold boxes
Of all shapes and sizes.
She showed people
The spacious rooms,
The possible possibilities.
She opened windows and doors
To the many who called her.

But one day, aged twenty-five,
The windows and doors closed.
Her world became small and dark
And for eight days she entered hell.
A realm that she was not prepared for,
A realm she did not deserve.
Her hopes and happiness were stolen
Her present and future crushed
And discarded like compacted trash.

And when all of the surviving pieces of Stephanie
Were allowed to leave the house of horrors,
She was re-cycled back into normality
Into a clean and comforting world.
But sadly and inhumanely,
She was still treated like dirt.

And so much of her sad story remained hidden
Inside her buried box,

Too afraid to open up,
Too damaged to move on.

In her own time she made changes,
To run away from her past,
To start a new present,
To find a future.

But as her years slowly doubled
She was given a new life sentence,
A brief contract of eleven days
And when that ended
She returned
To her dark and
Breathless
Box.

To Natalie Ward (1978-2006)

Natalie, a hair stylist, died on a pedestrian crossing, struck by a car driven by a pensioner with very little eye sight. She was shopping for her wedding dress.

Natalie followed the code,
She enjoyed school, work and family life,
Her glass was full of bubbles,
But she walked the straight and narrow.
She was to be married
In six months' time.
Save the day.

She brought life and laughter
To any party,
She brought love and laughter
To her partner,
She was to be married
In six months' time.
Save the day.

Natalie was a vision of beauty,
And yet in the mirror she stood
In the background,
Interested in everyone else,
Praising and reassuring all,
Reflecting her personality
With a smile and a story.
She was to be married
In six months' time.
Save the day.

So, Natalie took her mother
Shopping for a wedding dress.
Not a hair out of place
Without a care in the world,
But still aware of others.
They followed the code,
Natalie in front, taking the lead,
For once in her life.
They were looking forward
To the day.

And then it hit them,
The beast that can't see beauty
In anything and anyone.
The mother spared,
The daughter died.

Natalie passed on Valentine's Day.
Save the day,
Please, save the day.

To Judee Sill (1944-1979)

Judee, one of the greatest singer/songwriters in America, battled through a short but turbulent life of drug addiction, prostitution, ill health and crime to create an anthology of beautiful songs. She died in obscurity from a drug overdose. No obituary was written at the time of her death.

She was a dark star
Living and dying in the shadows
Of helplessness and hopelessness.

A half-life lived alongside
Abuse and abusers
Looking for peace and light
At the end of her brief tunnel.

But her stop-start journey was punctuated
By songs of elusive love and peace,
Beautiful notes to feed the heart,
Which kept the monsters in line
And the devils temporarily at bay.

She played unhappy families,
She played on the mean streets,
And prayed for forgiveness
In-between the highs and the lows.

But no-one listened,
No-one bought into her music,
No-one came to her rescue.

She was a lost and fading child.
Her life and death shrouded in
A conspiracy of silence,
A mystery of obscurity,
A lack of care.

Her long suffering has ended
Far too soon,
And we now bear her cross.

To Lidia Dragescu (1994-2017)

Lidia, a talented medical student, web site designer, poet and figure skater, committed suicide by throwing herself off the Whispering Gallery at St. Paul's Cathedral. She was clutching two notes of apology as she fell – one to her mother and one to the people who witnessed her fall.

"Beautiful falling angel
Don't leave us
For a better place,
Don't leave us
To escape."
(St.Paul implored from the floor)

"But I cannot wait any longer
To see what's on the other side
I am doing this for myself
With a heavy heart and head."
(Lidia whispered from the gallery)

"But you are just a child in my eyes
With so much more to give,
You are a Renaissance woman
With so much more to learn.
Knowledge is your duty."
(St.Paul pleaded from the floor)

"It is too late for me to learn
That I can fly.
My wires are crossed
And I am dancing on thin ice.

Please note -
I am sorry."
(Lidia replied)

"Lidia, Lidia
There will be a second coming,
I promise you.
We will pray for you,
God Bless You."
(St.Paul prayed as he knelt on the floor)

To Christine Keeler (1942-2017)

Christine Keeler, a young woman trying to make her way in the world in the late 1950s and early 1960s, was caught up in a political scandal and was shoddily treated by the hypercritical establishment then and afterwards.

A child in a different time
A plastic model stuck in her prime,
Left naked and exposed
Used, abused and spat out
By established older generations
Who knew better.

A poor girl, abandoned,
Trying to escape poverty,
Working hard to find
Love, kindness, acceptance.

Stumbling into a dark world,
She was prodded and poked
By accusing fingers.
The target of slings and arrows,
The naïve victim,
The sin collector.

Imprisoned by the lies,
Public eyes looked down
And the shutters were closed,
Leaving only the image
Of a moment in time.
And as other moments passed,
She was never able to

Escape the myth or
Re-invent herself
With comforting security.

She was left in obscurity,
A different name
And a loving closed family.
The times turned,
Her pendulum swung,
The climate changed
From hot to warm,
From cool to cold.

The child was lost
In amongst the smoke and mirrors,
Killing her in the end and in the beginning,
Because no one wanted
To hear the rest or the best
Of Christine.

To Heather Heyer (1985-2017)

Heather, a paralegal from Virginia, was killed by a vehicle deliberately driven into a group of counter demonstrators crossing the road who were opposing the activities of a white supremacy rally in Charlottesville.

We take a position
On one side or the other
Of a two-way street,
And look left and right.

In time,
As the road widens
And the traffic increases,
We are too scared to move,
Too entrenched to cross.
So, we stay safe and secure
By looking right or left.

One day,
We may meet in the middle,
But for now we call across the road
Shouting warnings.

So, no-one approaches
The middle ground
Untravelled, uninhabited.
And the road turns to grey
And blurs the black and white.
But as others join you on the sidewalks,
You are tempted on to the front line
And having decided,

You take a side,
The right side
And cross.

But you were stopped in your tracks.
You fell where you stood,
You stood where you fell.

We all knew where you stood,
Heather.
We all know why you fell,
Heather.

Please stop.

Last Poem

This is the last poem
In the book,
I'm sure you will be pleased to know.
It has taken much paper and ink
As well as much time to think
About the chosen words I need to use
To produce this last poem.

So, sadly, this is the last page
In this book,
There may not be another page
Of another book,
There may not be anybody to read
The future truth,
As the music is fading from our ears
And the light is dimming in our eyes.

So, this is the last poem on Earth
You will ever want to read.

IAN MEACHEAM

Ian Meacheam spent most of his working life in education. He was a teacher of English and Drama in secondary schools in Solihull. He then became a school improvement advisor in Birmingham working for the local authority. His first novel, "An Inspector Called" revolves around a secondary school in the aftermath of an Ofsted inspection. His first poetry anthology, "Stone People Glass Houses" reflects on the many contrasts in our lives, in a serious and not so serious way.
Ian lives in Lichfield with his wife Ann. They have one son, David.

VERSE FROM APS PUBLICATIONS
(www.andrewsparke.com)

Artists 4 Syria (Various)
Broken English (Andrew Sparke)
Close But Not Close Enough (Lee Benson)
Dub Truth (Kokumo Noxid)
Every Picture Hides A Friend (Lee Benson)
Failing To Be Serious (Lee Benson)
Fractured Time (Andrew Sparke)
Gutter Verse & The Baboon Concerto (Andrew Sparke)
Jottings and Scribbles (Lee Benson)
Meandering With Intent (Lee Benson)
Refracted Light (Andrew Sparke)
Shining Lights Dark Matters (Ian Meacheam)
Silent Melodies (Andrew Sparke)
Stone People Glass Houses (Ian Meacheam)
The Gathering (Malachi Smith)
The Highwayman, Pink Carnations and The Re-Allocated Coal Scuttle (Revie)
Vital Nonsense (Andrew Sparke)
Walking The Edge (Various)
Wicked Virtue (Andrew Sparke)

Printed in Poland
by Amazon Fulfillment
Poland Sp. z o.o., Wrocław